BLACK DOG

ACKNOWLEDGMENTS:

I would like to thank the editors of the following journals where some of these poems first appeared:

The New Republic, Ploughshares, Menhaden Press, South Dakota.

NOTES

Black Dog; 1706, a cant name for a base silver coin. 1826, a depression of spirits; ill humor. Vernacular Scots-Irish usage, according to *Oxford Universal Dictionary on Historical Principles,* Little and Onions, editors, 1933.

BLACK DOG

Poems • Margo Lockwood

margo lockwood

*for Callan B Cqnole
with neighborly rue!*

Alice James Books
Cambridge, Massachusetts

Publication of this book was made possible with support from the National Endowment of the Arts, Washington, D. C. and from the Massachusetts Council on the Arts & Humanities, a state agency whose funds are recommended by the Governor and appropriated by the State Legislature.

Library of Congress Catalogue Card Number 86-080007
    ISBN   0-914086-60-X (cloth)
    ISBN   0-914086-61-8 (paper)

Alice James Books are published by the Alice James Poetry Cooperative, Inc.

Alice James Books
138 Mount Auburn Street
Cambridge, Massachusetts 02138

CONTENTS

LANDFALL

Eroding like a beached stone, a moon
pared itself away. Glasgow, it had
its fullness; Larne, a little less;
Stranraer, gibbous.

Crossing to Ulster, the shudder
at landfall made me clutch
at the woman next to me on the bench,
ask her if it was a bomb.

A pipers' convention skirled
& squealed around, and drunken
families. I could hardly hear.

But anxiety is so familiar there
she pressed her flat key on me.
"My street is fairly safe," rrrrr's rolling
the "fairly" more archaic than Scotch.

At the gangway, ammunition-girted
men wanded me through; black plastic sticks
purring at certain mixtures
of chemical and metal,

go silent at shoes, books, underwear,
the odd crystal flask of new perfume,
or smuggled whiskey.

I hope the familiar will come back,
the black sky through strange lace
will seem the velvet jewel box of the stars,
not this movie set, searchlights all night,

a sinister ocean lapping Ireland,
the damp and homey menace.

ULSTER TELEVISION

I meant to be neutral
until I saw the doors
battered with axes
and the windows gone.

I thought the town would be
just a town, fountains, public buildings,
throngs of shoppers, drinkers in the pubs.

The party walls between houses
stood, their fireplaces open to the sky;
and groups of men in caps and overcoats
no more than three at time,
walked down the middle of what used
to be the street.

Mourners — the next-of-kin
are interviewed at supper on tv.
They are impressed by their own
notoriety, even as they grieve in public.

The cause stains through their words —
exposed to the viewer
even as they talk, and their sons dead.

Something has split the common tongue
so that the Lord of Misrule holds two sticks.
The guessing game is short. The choice is
one side or the other.

DUBLIN STREETS

Always shining with rain, its aftermath
or prescient with it — umbrella people
natty in sun, but shelter always at the ready.

Lovers are folded around each other
under gazebos and pavilions in Stephen's Green —
in the lee of the wind behind statues —

face on face, the only parts dry
the parts of their bodies that touch
in a hot oblivion, surprising me.

Narrow clerks take back streets at a run,
thin-shouldered in tight checks, pencilling
the bed-sit pages when they light in cafés

then leaving their lists in phone booths
all over the north side, near the zoo
where they and I and the lovers all go

for comic relief from the city streets,
brick Georgian squares, and cobbled walks
where a roughness of money aches to be spent —

far from the fan-lights and stately gray
façades and rococo plaster ceilings
prized for their height and cold perfection.

YELLOW DAY LIKE A STILL LIFE

On the table landscape
of my desolate kitchen
in the middle of Ireland
in the bleary damp of spring —

butter rises like a greasy fort
from a saffron yellow saucer.

A washcloth, pale yellow,
is folded as a miniature tent
over the toys the children ranged,
militia-like, around their breakfast.

Doorways in Fitzwilliam Square
bear brass shields worn & shiny,
from charladies' polish for a century.

Their gold shines
in the brittle monstrance
of the rare sunlight.

My lips taste only of lemon drops.
No longer any vestiges of your own.

THE SPORT

At a tap on the kitchen window
fronting the sea, my heart pounded.
A robber, a tinker, is it?
I opened the iron latch −

then the big bar sliding free
to a cold night
and my own surprise.

The bitter, smart man −
the pilot, the man
of the mean aside.

He puts himself against the metal radiator.
"The back is out tonight."
Careless proud laugh that athletes
laugh at their injuries
that I know from my brothers, my sons.

I can't imagine his world.
Civil servant chaff, the country farm,
cruelties of friendly gossip at the Arts Club,
rolling out of townhouses all over the city.

Breakfast under panels of hotel grille rooms,
where horsemen & farmers sit,
tall windows giving onto 18th century thoroughfares,
broad enough for six carriages abreast.

And I can't imagine my life
when I won't stand in Dublin
waiting for my bus, pearly sky
roiling past in the downpour air.

Loneliness around my throat
like a pearl choker.

USES OF THE ATLAS

Ireland's 4 million population
means it will be all that much harder
to run into him.

If I go to the West,
few there
to remind me.

Waiting for my bus on the quay
I can break silence like hard bread
chatting with strangers about weather.

I won't always have
this waterfall adrenalin
pushing me around.

Or be a Samuel Beckett woman,
sad-sack in weathery tweeds.

I can see myself poring
through atlases in libraries
all over the world −

estimating the distance
I need to keep me away
from his side.

TURF-STACKING

When neighbors showed me how to stack the turf,
they said a little thing under their breath:
"Two tall towers for the little church,
and a half stone for the top where the cross
sits, so." And put a wax cube, paraffin,
a *firelighter* up there.

I raise and let fall the poker,
stirring vestigial heat
and constellations of carbon stars
bloom like lichen on the back
of the fire wall.

Here in the midden heap of the world,
Barrow of Celts, of the Passage Grave people,
where cathedrals stood a millenium ago,

I picnic in the ruin of one, next to
my traffic *roundabout*.

130 words for love in Old Irish,
and the 17 alphabet letter names
bear the gaelic names of trees.

"Alim, Beith, Kill, Dare.
Elm, Beech, Elder, Oak."

And roses, salted by the sea,
survive past Christmas.

ON EDGE

Ice hardly ever forms in Ireland
yet I am skating on it,
and it's thin.

Sitting through a bombscare
in a travel agency, the manager
proffers chocolates; we pass them
around like aperitifs. "If we go,
we go on a full stomach."

We peer through plate glass,
though the illusion of *inside*,
as soldiers wheel the might-be-bomb
onto O'Connell Street in a lead box.

Tall blue men on watch cross themselves.
At the sign of the cross, the crowd,
cordoned off two blocks away, all cheer.
They're always cheering here.

For farmers on parade, trade unionists
on walk-out, bareback processions
of tinkers on strike for maternity care.

It would be hard here,
if it weren't for the cheering –
and lack of ice.

FULL FEBRUARY MOON

Under a sky torn by clouds, I sigh
sotto voce, waiting at the bus stop
on the Monkstown Road.

A false spring. Cherry blossoms leap
through the stone wall's broken place,
the break occasioned

by the Great Wind of '74
when the oaks all came down,
and this road was filled
with green tree-tops for a week.

This particular cherry tree —
split down the middle, comes
into flower early, ever since.

It reminds me of my daughters,
dancing in Dublin through the night,
fifteen and seventeen,
their magenta tights & pink silk
scarves blown from the laundry line

to tear against the stone wall
of the garden, like the pink
of these cherry blossoms.

Shrubs all along
this broken wall bend,
then reap the sleet
clustered beneath tall beech,
hesitant rowan.

If they haven't been otherwise damaged,
their season isn't upon them yet,

and they hold the pale greenwood to come
at bay with skeletal arms.

I felt like switching their legs
with the branches I stole
and brought home.

But they only took the blossoms
and pinned them in their hair.

HALF-SUN

I turn from the mirror to the garden
where the December rose grows up orange
above the wall.

Soughing the grasses chinked in and
threaded on its top — the wind
displaces the still life of a great turf,
like Dürer's.

The great gray rain comes slanting down
interrupting the museum in my eyes.

Ars brevis, sometimes, when the day
holds out only a magdalene of a cabbage rose,
loosening itself to the wind, like a slattern
at her laundry line.

RAINBOW AT TWO O'CLOCK

Back-lit, the sea receives the rainbow's end.
A band of jade slants through the blue
refracting everything it hits.

As if to surfeit this excess in Dublin Bay
a school of winter-coat white gulls
is wheeling at their midday feast
in the descending prism

their wings at every angle
like white Ogham runes
against the gray slate air.

There needs to be menace in the sky
a feeling of shipwreck in the sea
then it will show up, like a virgin
in a circus parade.

Gaga with optical effects, men slow
on their bicycles. In vans and trucks
the traffic stops. The populace
like a primitive tribe stands
at the wrought-iron fence
above the seaside.

At the telephone booth on the road
a man ringing his mistress on his lunch
break hangs up. *Darling, I have to go.*
There is a rainbow.

GAZE

A month gone by, and days
like clouds form above
the sea. A man I met
smiled at me from a chair,
took my hand, talked to me simply.

When I turn in the warm bed
windowpanes, rain light,
and the garden whiten
under the moon.

Memory colors me like a flush.
I lie on my thin bed where I
crowded him, where everything

is changed but my pillowslip
that I savor like an Elizabethan
dame would her gallant's glove.

Fetishes abound. My cells give back
his imprint like a negative.

I looked long at his mouth
smiling as he slept. It made me
take his careless hand.

BACK

I know I'm here because these are my hands
upon my knees. My eyes that stare
at wallpaper I put up
six years ago.

These bones
that lie across the old green couch
and tremble during the ten o'clock news,
my bones.

This is the way my ancestor-Irish-farmers
felt, coming in from the fields at dusk,

the fork in their hand at supper
a miniature of the pitchfork
they'd been hefting all day.

It had been my idea, going to Ireland.
But it took years to get home,
the debt mountain to climb –

borrowing from those tall,
stern relatives, my brothers –
"Being quixotic again, Mag?"

I don't have their knack for knowing
if it was worth it, rambling around Europe
on the cheap,

two children still clinging
to my sides like soft luggage.

Just something that I did,
and it changes things.
One takes that shuddering breath
and begins.

WIND FLOWERS

There were flowers all summer long
in my side pasture, anemones and poppies,
all the largesse of a place
tended a while.

I buy them
when I see them on the street
in tin buckets from those rough men,
the flower men.

There is so much black
I hadn't seen before
in their fast bloom
at the base of their brilliant throats.

When I stop, stock still
fishing out my coins
rooting for the change to keep their impatience
within bounds

I catch my breath
in the iron music of the street;
and feel like a fossil
in a burning museum.

BLACK DOG

I see my children learn
to lean away from me,
avoiding my anger with a grin
the wrong size.

And why not, I say,
who raised them up alone,
hoping that the wind
would temper to the shorn lambs?

Not in ways that would have them
grow too gentle though –
so that in their adulthood
there would be nothing common
to us all.

I see too many
soft in the wrong place
who flinch and yield
at every prod
who bury their face
in their hands
too often –

so that the gesture
loses its terrible purity.

HEALTH

The post office automatic writing system
I use to communicate with you,
my beloved dead, is getting fogged over.

It used to be that I couldn't have
a pencil in my hand
but that worlds would stain out, onto paper,
elegaic, melancholy.

Now I leave my baggage at home
and walk around this city
that I know like my old pair of boots,
too well, the scuffed apparatus of it.

There is a reason for this lightness.
I was starting to notice myself
breathing heavily.
You have moved away from me,
out into the starry worlds, I guess.

Memory is doing its encapsulation trick.
Your faces, the pores of your skin,
the liquidity, the hue of the iris of your eyes,
fade for me. I seek other,
living faces to take my pleasure with.

I make small prayers against unfaithfulness.
I hope, I trust, it is because
you loved, I loved you, well.
To the hilt,
to the bloody hilt,
I sometimes think.

OXFORD STREET MUSEUM

At eighteen when I worked in Öology,
in the Egg Room on the fifth floor,
stabled above the door that read
"Nabokov: Entomology"
where we looked at tarantulas
all during lunch —

nature, far from being in me,
or something I was "of,"
was the courtyard I walked down into,

the air a relief from formaldehyde
soaking through the bodies
of the dead animals, mounted
in crowded Victorian cases.

Autumn air, or snappy chill snow-speckled
air, or oozing lavender spring air
was nature or the beginnings of it.

The study that fogged the air deep
inside, was all Latin or Greek to me.
Nomenclature, species-differentiation —

I was a good speller, but that
was it, as far as science went.

Science was a country where I went to work,
as if into a war zone.
My life, however, was another question.
As real as my skin, my hair
the dynasties of DNA molecules
for which I was the Egg Room.

ISLAND SUMMER

The first child lay
on the drying sheets spread over
the tall grass, so we could see
the ticks, if they came crawling.

We stood over him, in sailor pants
that buttoned up, that we found in the cottage chests,
unopened after the World War.

Thin as courtship's hard work
and the 20 x 40 garden had made us.

The pump stood akimbo in the yard,
and sometimes the soon-to-be-dying
grandmother went and tried her hand at it,
in proud, plump, muscle-heaving plunges.

The days stretched ahead like new cloth,
with no flaw or speck,
the cool wind bringing fog
over the fields like clockwork
every afternoon at four,

so that one had to be aware of the passing hours
as husbandry for the first time.

I drank the summer in as if it was my right and due
but dangerously, as if it were
supposed to last that way,
in storage for my sweet content,

and the months ticked by
like a clock maintained by crickets.

NUN

Not meaning to,
I've lived like a nun
in a nun's world.

Dun brown the tree trunks,
dull gray the water
at the Reservoir
where I walked the asphalt paths.

I disliked being a young
widow. Thirty seemed too raw,
a curio.

When I laughed too much
at parties did people think
I was a merry one?

Exhaust on the street was harsh
from trucks. I knew sea air
was blowing up Route Nine
above the traffic
all the time.
It was the prevailing wind.

I was being as happy as I knew
how. I wanted to do the job
without distortion, or complaint.

That is the black ground
of the canvas. I knew that darkness
is a place to start from
when you're stymied by
blank white.

The funeral of Tillie McDonnell
was held on a chill bright day.
Nothing up, the grass a memory
of green in the brown hummocks.

Old Irish ladies' hands gripped mine,
and then returned to their pews,
gnarly as dockers' — blue eyes in plain
faces, shy as school girls.

"In Service" they were.
The euphemism for that kind of life,
Tillie's life.

Refusing a ride to the cemetery
I hoofed a mile and a half to work.

The smarmy priesty talk
had taken my appetite
away for inevitable pastel
sandwiches, dry sugar cookies,
the thin bright orange tea
at Tillie McDonnell's
aprés burial party.

Sometimes it's convenient to be moody.
Let them figure I am affected by the day.
Forget that I ever came by
the stodgy church, its smell
of holiness that's only
Butcher's Wax.

Hand-wringing men in lace cassocks!
Those hands too soft and puffy
that shook mine. Their only exercise
turning the car wheel in parking lots
of seafood restaurants.

NOËL MINIMAL

Spring is contained in the chill
snow egg of nature. Its coiling
green can't figure out
how to die.

From my upstairs window
I can make out, even at midnight
twelve different steeples needling
the sky, and white barn roofs,
trapezoids, pitches, mansards,

all simplified because all
snowy – through white lace curtains.

There's more than glass
between the lace and the snow.

The cement garden statue, K'wan Yin,
has an unsettled beatitude in falling
snow. She'll be obscured by roses, come June.
The way she always was in my mother's
last garden.

VINTAGE CLOTHES

I saw a man in the neighborhood,
the neighborhood of my life.
Walking, a charming smile –
grey jacket, and thought, Do I know
that face?

It was the old grey jacket I liked,
its careless retrograde chic.
By little things, our fancy moves.

I took a few walks with him.

And all fall, yellow leaves hung
longer on the trees, unseasonal spring
air forced forsythias to false bloom.

Hilarious – all the prematurity!
And now frost is here. And tomorrow
promises of snow.

SMALL SONG

'Unless I calm my blood
and my soul, how shall I live?"

Great Song, Li Ho (791-817 A.D.)

Twisted into a question mark,
I sat by the highway
waiting for my blood to stop
hammering in my throat.

Too flushed to go into a store
and my pink shirt had a few spots
of blood from your passion-thwarting
nosebleed.

You mock me with a formal goodbye,
and go down that road to see a friend.
Now proper, not with lake water
dripping from your forehead.

I went on eventually
and bought two peach trees.
How Chinese I feel
these days.

MEDITATIVE AFTERNOON

Young men up on ladders
painting buildings
in the sunlight on the south wall
with all the shadows
of the ladders and their bodies

their spring skin tanning up fast

it is enough to make one
falter in one's resolve
to make art count.

But there were days on the river grass –
dallying with a sorrel stalk tossing
in the cupped hands rubbing back & forth
with young men just like this –

and all I could think of
was wit and barb, keeping the balance,
and them at bay for the game's sake,
the appropriate delay

all in the unendingness of summer.

BLUE WILLOW

The K'wan Yin floats
above the garden bushes
now that it's May.

Her cement robes
granular and gray;
at her feet, pebbles,
and the scree of years,
weathering.

Small violets with angle-iron stems
low to the earth among the stones;
white ones with black veins;
purple ones more commonplace
like cheap women, brighter
in church than the others.

I wanted to leave that petal world,
world where I was doomed to notice just
what was small.

Something about you
made me think
of the willow ware design.

A blue man that a blue lady
runs to. Birds, stylized & Persian,
flying by on the vault of Heaven.
Mid-heaven in the saucer.

Is it just to be entering
the myth world I fell in love?
. . . time passing in slipper-feet
if it wasn't barefoot?

Or was I in it, in my life
with children, awkward simple
life, and have fallen
from it now?

AUGUST THUNDER

Sometimes the room is just a box
of yellow light, morning coming in
through the gray tablecloth tacked up,

so that the day
is half thundercloud,
half ordinary.

Or a flickering cave
where we dispose ourselves – old lamp
in an alcove, the small fire of a fireplace
we can't quite see.

One August night, your departure
looming like clouds, or alps,
two thunderstorms crossed Boston.

The first seemed the usual for August,
but the second woke me hard.

A terror of angelic hosts, crashing
fanfaronades above my head.
One second, two – at least two miles away.

Lethal light yields to the feral sound.
Ozone, diamond rain, a thousand
drops per cubic foot! I make up
scientific wonders to explain my life.

Maybe I should have wished
that lightning to come in
and strike so we could have died
in that happiness I couldn't imagine fading.

Now I feel I was burning
thousand-dollar bills in the dark
just to see your face.

EXILE

After you came back
we walked to the Brookline Reservoir,
ice underfoot and snow,
leaves eroded to their veins
like the stunned workings of a clock,
after so long.

How apt we each wore black.

Everything now is something
I'm forbidden to do
by a prior woman to me,
and probably others too.

Ice moaned as its plate grew
thicker near the shore. Thermodynamics
at work, like entropy.
I can apply that to you.

Whales' songs sound like that;
the octave they moan in
has a great low C like the ice
when it moves its disconsolate whole,
trying to freeze more.

Inanimate universe, water and stone,
tolling, even such a thing as ice
trying to warn. That's how I took it,
anyway.

Your delicate accent positioned me,
sun blinded, and I smiled.
Out to the place with the camera
where you wheeled, out
on the icy planet, Self.

A QUESTION OF SCALE

Blackberries behind spiderwebs
ripen in a hot wind, hovering
between tart & rot.

Ripening takes weeks.
The corollas of berries ripen
from the edges, in.

High wind worries the boughs
in which bitter apples
streak to pink
along their yellow globes.

Dark bells begin to sound
and chill nights catch the hooks
of the first regardless leaves.

And you're gone.

Days shorten,
narrow in their band of sun.
They feel a week long,
every one.

When you come back
we'll picnic on a field
as big as the Northeast.

That acreage will barely contain
our arms & legs. Berries will stain
our backs, small thorns embed
themselves on freckles
left from summer.

Huge again,
not small-scale imitations
of ourselves.
I will shrink
only while you're away.
Less of me
to feel anything.

THE HAPPY WORLD

Is what I've won
the mild regard
in the golden iris
of your eyes

as I laboriously trek
from the old stove with Hollywood-style
black & creme designs

to the round table
that tilts with the slanting floor?

There are things
I can't forget
in the happy world.

Oh, I was the abject one.
Reading the anorexic theology
you'd press on me, to see
if I'd perhaps assent
to a bodiless friendship

something like William Blake
suggested to his uncomplaining wife?
I always said no.

Oh, I was a hard-working one.
Baking flawless breads, no sugar
or syrup, only barley malt —
in the narrow spectrum
you'd permit.

Flames from candles I lit
fall over in Phoenix candlesticks
always unsteady, ever since
my dead husband bought them,
in a faded blue barn – the only
anniversary he bothered to remember.

Candles extinguish themselves
in flowers & water from tip-bottom
vases that fall when the candles do.
Home – a beautiful place, but unsteady,
askew.

Angular windows curl around corners.
Crystals wink in panes of old windows;
glass on glass, light on light, true love
on true love.

Chagall people floating in blue
forests, or is it just we two?
Oh, I was the hopeful one.

PEACHTREE PRAYER

Behind the little Chinatown
the Chin's trees, the Li's trees,
peach trees, reach pink fingertips
to the Mission Hill sky.

Children swarm in Sunday pajamas.

Maybe this hill is growing holy
as if a lumpish Buddhist goddess
within it is being entreated by prayer wheel
bicycles and Chevy hubcaps.

Magic any old way takes place
when a limousine brings a storekeeper
from big Chinatown to this backyard
to have his ankle cured by Mrs. Li.

Spotlights shine down summer nights.
He can't hop up the three flights
to her kitchen, so the neighborhood
looks down through parted laundry
as she pulls & kneads the swelling.

At the finish, everybody claps.
It is a community cure.

Maybe some night I will bring
my heart and she will lessen its
fullness, under a waning
or a beginning moon.

AUSTRIAN CHRISTMAS MAIL

The air between us yawns
like a sheer drop. So many mountains.
Land between, pleated.
Young alps and appenines shrug
their bony shoulders
under the Christmas stars.

Twice I called Vienna.
Roaring transatlantic cables
carried weird silences
we pay a half month's rent for;
to breathe into each other's ears
in *real* time.

A cryptic letter for Christmas,
Österreich stamps; ". . . in the air above
our rooftops, Brookline Village,
the Opera neighborhood of Vienna, something. . .
disembodied, platonic, meets."

So noncommittal, it sounds like you're
afraid of blackmail, in the city
where spies cross like railroad tracks.

The formal quality you prefer
casts a black & white harlequinade
over my wintry scenes.

I keep saying goodbye,
shaking your hand in the way of pilgrims.
Wondering how much more
I can jettison
in these partings,
then returning
over so many kinds of distances.

COUNTRYSIDE NEAR PEMBROKE, MASSACHUSETTS

There were days in November
when I was a young, a lonely mother —
driving country roads
stopping here for bread,
there for geraniums;

shifting in pain to nurse
a baby on the front seat
of my truck.

The stubble of corn
shone like blonde hair.

I got to know
roadside stands

contours of towns
where I knew no people.

In flight daily from a bitter man's
love, or lovelessness, my stomach
knotted up.

Young girls with babies often spend

hours near railroad track cafés,
drinking coffee to go;

where the feed store's red & white sign
is the enlargement of the oilcloth
tabletop checkers.

The warmth of discourse
with unirritated strangers
lets one mull one's condition
like a juggler,

at the quick of experience,
miles from desire or sadness.

ARTIST SON

Scion, first-born boy,
burdened with firstness –
I come upon a drawing
that you did for me years back,
under a pile of bills on the dresser.

On ruled paper, in graphite number two –
my favorite English vase, with a yellow vine
traipsing around it – familiar weeds
from the backyard plumped out
to fill in the ratty bouquet.

A semi-circle of café au lait, my mark,
there, on some unravelling edges
that show it ripped from your
high school notebook.

I call across the generation
that sails between us like a front
of weather, angling the entire sky,

mouthing the few commandments I have kept
hoping you hear me in spite of the noise
made by everything else.

HAND-CARRIED WATER

To get more air, I sit on the rooftop
on a folding chair, the gravel
like goldgrit, even the leaves
of the trashtree, ailanthus,
yellow in this sun

that cannot reach my friend
in her meticulous dying
in a hospital right down the street.

And I had been complaining
of a lack of water
for my kitchen work.
Bitching at my son
while he learned plumbing,
torching away beneath the sinks.

Each morning all month
I carried water up two flights
and watched the pitchers empty
as we poured ourselves clean
for the day.

The water in glass jugs
blue green and brimming —
glowed as if lit
from within

taking on the color
in the glass
that one can't see unless
it's full.

The amber days are on a chain.
A chain with my name on it.

BACKWARD-WALKING WOMAN

I liked walking backwards, up the highway,
watching the heaps of Hollywood clouds,
sunset tincturing them.

Sunset! and you were just dawning on me.

I walked beside you like a solitary
hermit, or a nun. But we
had made that sculpture
out of our tired limbs,
slaking ourselves at the fountain
that spills over us, that is
our bodies' body.

For a long time, I just wondered about you.
At the shore line all I saw
was moss, wildflowers and distance.

My island self erected ladders and beacons,
lookout stations, unaware while building,
that there might be such a word as NO.
It was a game. Blind man's bluff
with ghosts.

But I am revising my past, my sins,
deconstructing my novel life story.
I will walk backwards, kiss by kiss,
until I come to my funny childhood,
virtuous and unmagdalenic –
and I will end, beginning again, with you.

ALBUM

Irish castles, falling to their knees,
collapsing in the saturated light
in grass that looks white
in the wind, early Easter grass
like hair too frail for the comb.

In unkempt keeps
sheep wander through –
the slattern gates ajar.

I stood in a lancet window,
a dolmen effigy in the wreck of a church.

My mother was taking the picture.
That was a funny coat
I wore – when I was thirty five.

She cut my feet off
to get the ruin of the the church in.
Her way.

And what will he do with the pictures
he's taking of me?

There will have to be albums
no one sees.

Who will know him that knew me
where he goes? What reason
will there be
for opening
my page?

GRAY PARIS

Tall as a queen's effigy
in blackened stone
Paris stood round me.

Spring was being kept indoors;
each salon a tiny court
where winter flowers ruled;
where fine lawn curtains
kept the public out.

Phrases from novels
stood in shadows
behind buildings, tricks
my education had
taught me to see.

I was gloveless in Paris & stung
my hands on the cold of wrought-iron gates;
their pattern left a chilblain fleur-de-lys
on my palm that healed by the time
of the Calais boat to Ireland.

I rubbed my hands like a navvy
over the green waves. We shrugged
our way through cliffs; stiff granular
sugar battlements, the harbor's hooks

like epaulets on the shoulders of France.

France, chill and imperious
but in whose history I play
a speck of a part.

My spirit flies like a gray pigeon
to my uncle's grave at Saint Lo.
Since Normandy his place.
A patch under a stoic soldier's cross,
white wood.
Weathering in all weather.

So many crosses on those acres,
looking makes the eyes too dry for tears.

SPRECHSTIMME

I stand up in the summer air
picking the first windfalls
underneath the dwarf pear.

My children, somewhere else
for a change, and my husband
and now my mother, dead, and
in this light
everything particle-heavy and clear,
and sudden in its present tense.

So I spread the drying sheets
beneath my head and nap
on the dull green grass,

while the apple branches
hold the afternoon away
from me on tenterhooks

and I know all around the neighborhood
white-haired women are tracking
their way to church for the 4:00
benedictions.

A subtle honey
purrs into the comb –
the tiny hymn of insect
industry

the only work or clock,
and my slow pencil
is their metronome.

MILK WOMAN INTO STEEL

Years and years
of being mild
have not affected me.

I'm starting out again
an angry woman, still milky
with children
but time is with me.

Time formerly a tapemeasure
with which I awaited
the rising of dough, or
of the moon

is now not merely
the number of hours
between the last child's
dropping off to sleep,
and my own.

I have learned
where flowers grow
for which I haven't
had to pay, neighborhood
stands of parsley, chives,
or tarragon, there
for the rifling.

Dispassionate
I look again at pictures
taken of our family when
you were still alive,
children with incipient faces
breaking through their infancy,

and recognize I have grown cool
in my mold shaped like a dressmaker's form,

and stresses making it harder
& harder to change back again
work upon me like wind
destroying a bridge.

POETRY FROM ALICE JAMES BOOKS